Literacy and Language
Anthology
2 Book 3

Janey Pursglove and **Charlotte Raby**

Series developed by **Ruth Miskin**

Contents

OXFORD
UNIVERSITY PRESS

Chatterbox Ben

Adrian Bradbury

Monday morning, 9 o'clock, Class 2J

"Good morning, Martha."

"Good morning, Miss Johnson."

Miss Johnson put a neat tick in the register, against Martha's name.

"Good morning, Ashwin."

"Good morning, Miss Johnson."

Another precise tick.

"Good morning, Ben."

No answer.

"Has anyone seen Ben this morning?" Miss Johnson said, **peering** anxiously from table to table.

All the children shook their heads.

The clock ticked.

"Good morning, Sal—"

Crash!

The door burst open.

"I'm here, Miss Johnson, don't worry! Sorry I'm late, only the cat was sick all over the new white rug this morning and it took Mum ages to clear it all up. Then we had to take her to the vet…the cat that is, not Mum. We waited in a really long queue, and by the time the vet saw Bunger it was already half past eight…"

"That's OK. Just sit down now, please," said Miss Johnson.

"… And I said maybe I should stay at home today to look after Bunger, but Mum didn't seem keen on that idea, so here I am. Am I late? I hope not—"

"Enough!" Miss Johnson took a deep breath. She counted to ten. Then she forced a patient smile onto her face. "Good morning, Ben," she said sweetly.

Monday evening, Ben's bedroom

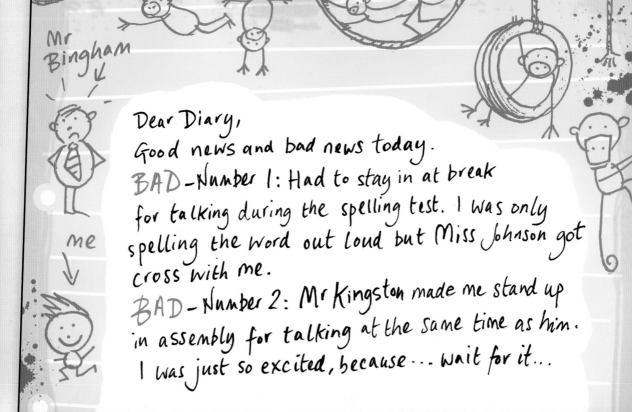

Mr Bingham

me

Dear Diary,
Good news and bad news today.
BAD – Number 1: Had to stay in at break for talking during the spelling test. I was only spelling the word out loud but Miss Johnson got cross with me.
BAD – Number 2: Mr Kingston made me stand up in assembly for talking at the same time as him. I was just so excited, because... wait for it...

GOOD NEWS

Mr Kingston told the school that to raise money to buy a school minibus he's planned a sponsored silence next week! How cool is that?! It'll be such a laugh, especially as it's the day after my birthday. The Quietest Class gets the reward of the first ride in the bus – to see the new zoo! I'll have to try really hard to stay silent. I know I talk a lot. I just can't help it! Night night.

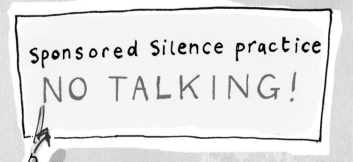

**Sponsored Silence practice
NO TALKING!**

Friday morning, 10 o'clock, Class 2J

In 2J's classroom, the children sat **hunched** over their books in silence, scribbling away at their stories. It was so quiet you could almost hear the scratch of pencils on paper. Zac put his hand up to ask Miss Johnson a question. Miss Johnson **glowered** at him and pointed to the sign on the wall. Zac bit his lip and reluctantly lowered his hand. In the back row, Martha was dying to sneeze. Her nose twitched like a rabbit's and her face was like a red balloon, ready to pop at any moment.

Everybody's lips were firmly sealed.

Well, *nearly* everybody's.

7

"This practice is a brilliant idea, Miss Johnson. I think we're doing really well. Even Martha's managed to hold in her sneeze. I didn't think I could keep silent, but I have, haven't I? We're bound to win the prize for the Quietest Class, aren't we, Miss Johnson?"

Miss Johnson's groan said it all.

Dear Diary,

What a fantabulous day this has been. Definitely my best ever birthday. Mum cooked my favourite lunch, then we had a huge chocolate cake and then the big surprise... Dad took me to watch United! They won 3-0. I've never cheered so much in my whole life! When I got home I just had to tell Mum all about it and sing her all the songs I learned from the United fans! Now I have to get a good night's sleep. Sponsored Silence tomorrow, and I don't want to let the class down. Night night.

Monday morning, 9 o'clock, Class 2J

sponsored silence
NO TALKING ALLOWED!

Miss Johnson waved at Lily. Lily waved back.

Tick.

Miss Johnson waved at Jacob. Jacob waved back.

Tick.

Miss Johnson waved at Ben. Her heart stopped beating, along with twenty-nine others. Twenty-nine heads **swivelled** towards Ben, and sixty eyes glared at him. He opened his mouth to answer.

Nothing came out.

He tried again.

Still nothing, not even a squeak.

Then he remembered the note. His hand reached out to Miss Johnson. She took the piece of paper and opened it up.

Dear Miss Johnson,

Please can you keep an eye on Ben today? Yesterday he was shouting and cheering so much at the football match that he gave himself a sore throat. This morning he seems to have completely lost his voice.

Yours sincerely,
Mrs Taylor (Ben's mum)

Miss Johnson waved at Ben.

Ben waved back.

Tick.

Thirty hearts started beating again. Miss Johnson beamed at the class. Twenty-nine children beamed back and breathed a silent sigh of relief.

Maybe 2J *would* be the Quietest Class after all.

And if they got to go to the zoo, Miss Johnson knew just the person to tell everyone about it in assembly!

Thrill City

To:	Jo Jones
Subject:	Totally Un-thrilling City!

Hi Jo!

Just got back from our class trip to Thrill City. What a nightmare – you'll never believe it! First, we went on the Spooky Train. There was this guy dressed as a skeleton, which I think was meant to be scary, but it really wasn't. We could see his trainers poking out under the bottom of the costume!

So I thought I'd go on the Big Wheel with Katie. But Knuckles Nick pushed in and I had to sit next to him instead. Then we got stuck right at the top for half an hour! When we finally got down, Nick said Miss Dixon had to call his mum because he was going to throw up! Yuck!

The Big Dipper worked but it wasn't very big and it didn't dip much! Oh yes – then we went for lunch, but Dan wasn't allowed in the café. He was soaked because one of his 'mates' had shoved him down the Super Slide. Miss Dixon tried to explain what happened to the staff but they wouldn't listen. The food was rubbish anyway and cost loads!

Letisha

Denton Dale Primary School
Brick Road
Denton

The Manager
Thrill City Theme Park
Epsom

12 July

Dear Sir or Madam,

I am writing to complain about our recent visit to your theme park. The trip was meant to be a reward for Class 2D's hard work, but it became more of a punishment!

Firstly, the theme park looked extremely old and run down. The students found both the rides and the special effects very disappointing.

Secondly, children were stranded when the Big Wheel broke down. One boy was so terrified he felt extremely unwell, and we had to ask his parents to come and collect him.

Finally, the quality of the food in your cafeteria was not acceptable. There were no healthy snacks available, the chips were cold and soggy and it was expensive. Also, one of your assistants was extremely unhelpful and rather rude to one of my teachers.

I hope that you will agree to refund the £12 entry price to each pupil.

Yours faithfully,

D. Hartley

Head teacher, Denton Dale Primary School

P.S. Photographs are enclosed with this letter to support our complaint.

Chocolate Planet

Jon Blake

The Planet Wob was a boring place. Nothing smelled tasty and nothing tasted of anything. Turnip fields stretched as far as the eye could see.

Gala was fed up with eating turnips. Every night she looked up at the Planet Um, hanging in the streaky sky. Everyone said there were chocolate mines on Um.

One evening, Gala was lying in a turnip field with her friend, Frag. The Planet Um was glowing a silky, milky brown.

Gala's mouth watered.
"Let's go there," she said.

"It could be dangerous," said Frag.

"It could be delicious," replied Gala.

"There could be scary things," said Frag.

"Nothing scares me," replied Gala.

As usual, Gala got her way. The two friends borrowed a spaceship from Rent a Rocket. They packed sky baskets, lunar bags and cosmic jars. Gala planned to harvest every last speck of chocolate.

It was a long journey to Um. Frag began to feel peckish. "Did you pack any food?" he asked Gala.

Gala produced two lovely round turnips.

"You shouldn't have bothered," moaned Frag.

At last the spaceship landed on the fudgy earth of Um. As soon as Gala and Frag opened the door they could smell chocolate. It was the most beautiful **aroma** in the universe.

"We have to follow that smell," said Gala. "It's sure to lead us to the chocolate mines."

Just then, a long, chilling howl filled the air.

"Was that...a moondog?" asked Gala.

"Probably," replied Frag.

Gala went as pale as a dust slug.

"I thought you weren't afraid of anything," said Frag.

"Nothing except moondogs," peeped Gala.

The howling grew louder. An awful panic took hold of Gala. Suddenly, from a nearby bush, the moondog sprang into view.

It was no bigger than a mouse. Seeing Gala and Frag, it ran for its life.

"I wasn't really scared," laughed Gala.

The two friends set off across Um, down wobbly paths of jelly stones, over winking streams of lemon water, till they saw a wall of galactic rock. The smell of chocolate was overpowering. Surely they had found the chocolate mines!

As they drew closer, however, they became aware of another smell. It was a nasty, musty smell, like the smell of a wet pet.

"I don't like that smell," said Gala.

"It's coming from that crack in the rock," said Frag.

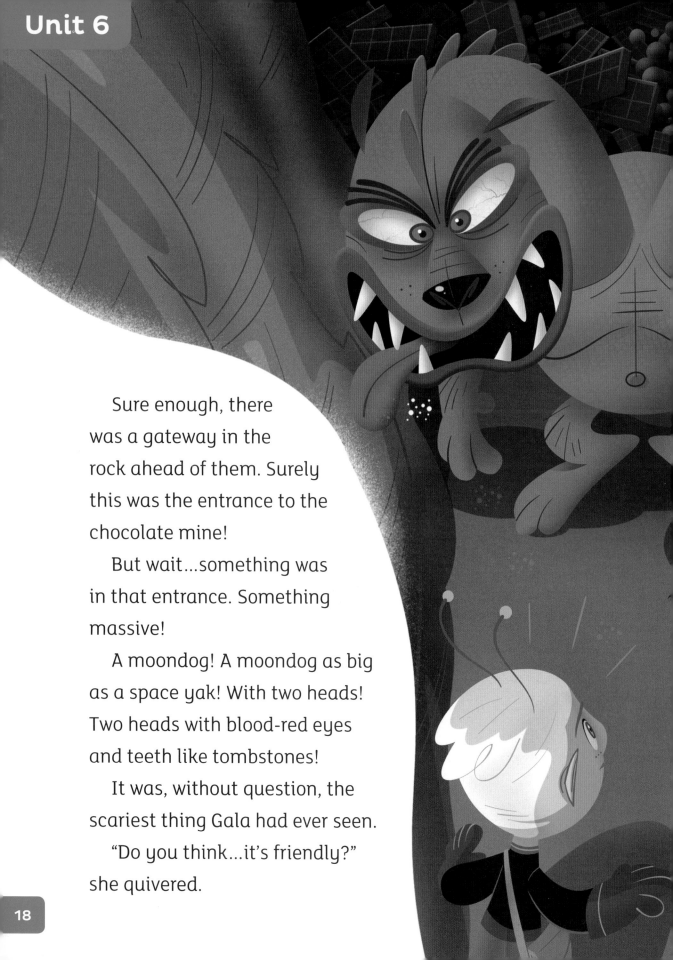

Sure enough, there was a gateway in the rock ahead of them. Surely this was the entrance to the chocolate mine!

But wait...something was in that entrance. Something massive!

A moondog! A moondog as big as a space yak! With two heads! Two heads with blood-red eyes and teeth like tombstones!

It was, without question, the scariest thing Gala had ever seen.

"Do you think...it's friendly?" she quivered.

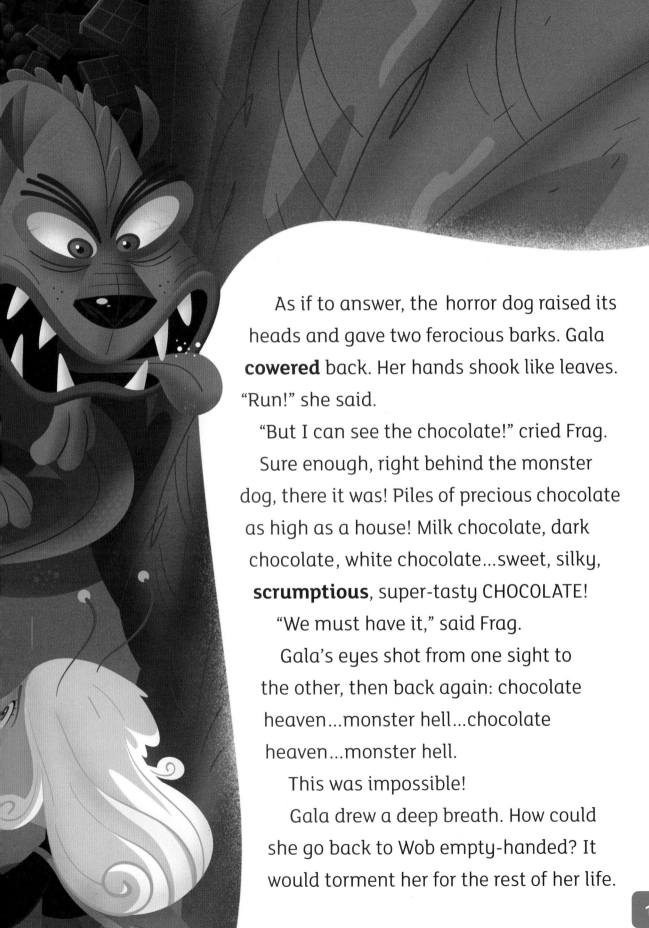

As if to answer, the horror dog raised its heads and gave two ferocious barks. Gala **cowered** back. Her hands shook like leaves. "Run!" she said.

"But I can see the chocolate!" cried Frag.

Sure enough, right behind the monster dog, there it was! Piles of precious chocolate as high as a house! Milk chocolate, dark chocolate, white chocolate...sweet, silky, **scrumptious**, super-tasty CHOCOLATE!

"We must have it," said Frag.

Gala's eyes shot from one sight to the other, then back again: chocolate heaven...monster hell...chocolate heaven...monster hell.

This was impossible!

Gala drew a deep breath. How could she go back to Wob empty-handed? It would torment her for the rest of her life.

Somehow, from somewhere, courage began to fill Gala's heart. Thinking calmly and clearly, she reached into her jacket and pulled out the two turnips she had brought. Holding on to one turnip, she handed the other to Frag. "When I shout," she said, "throw the turnip as hard as you can to the left."

Gala stood up tall so that the monster dog could clearly see her. "Here, boy," she said.

The moondog growled, a growl as deep as a crater. It took a **menacing** step towards her.

"Now FETCH!" cried Gala. She flung her turnip to the right.

Frag flung his turnip to the left.

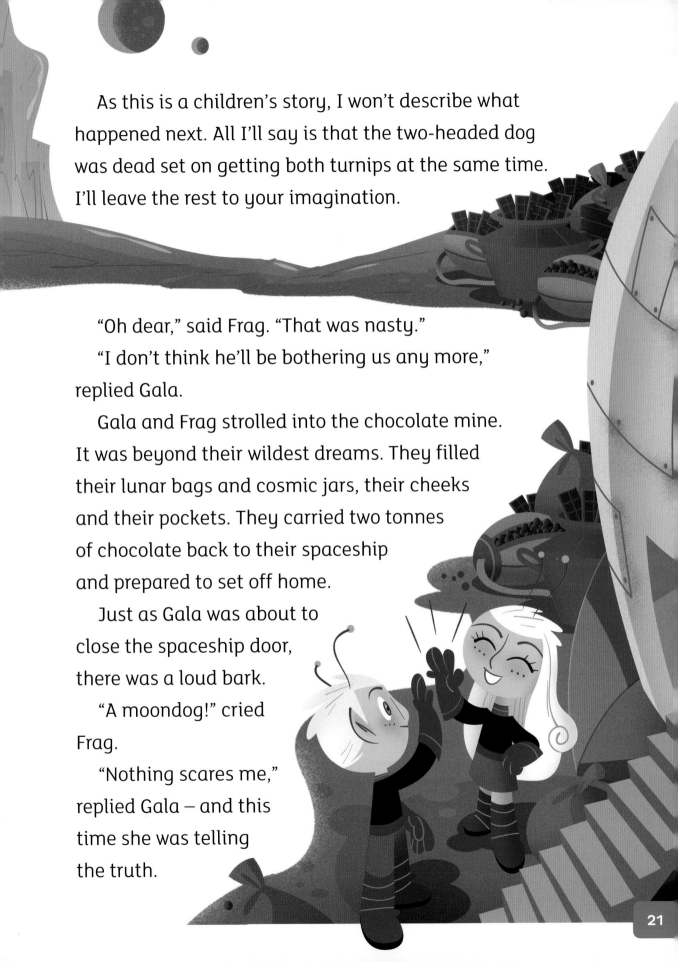

As this is a children's story, I won't describe what happened next. All I'll say is that the two-headed dog was dead set on getting both turnips at the same time. I'll leave the rest to your imagination.

"Oh dear," said Frag. "That was nasty."

"I don't think he'll be bothering us any more," replied Gala.

Gala and Frag strolled into the chocolate mine. It was beyond their wildest dreams. They filled their lunar bags and cosmic jars, their cheeks and their pockets. They carried two tonnes of chocolate back to their spaceship and prepared to set off home.

Just as Gala was about to close the spaceship door, there was a loud bark.

"A moondog!" cried Frag.

"Nothing scares me," replied Gala – and this time she was telling the truth.

Chocolate

Mad about chocolate? Find out how this top treat is made!

Where in the world?

Chocolate is made from cocoa beans, which grow on trees. These trees need warm, wet weather to grow. Mexico and Malaysia are good places for this, but most chocolate today is made from beans grown in West Africa.

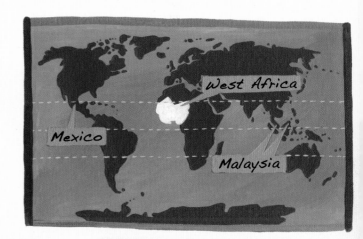

West Africa

Mexico

Malaysia

The history of chocolate

We know that people in Mexico were making a chocolate drink over 4,000 years ago. We think the name comes from an Aztec word that means 'bitter water'. It could be made more tasty by adding vanilla or chilli.

Spanish soldiers first tasted a chocolate drink in Mexico about 500 years ago. They liked it so much, they took some back to Europe.

Cocoa beans were used instead of money when people bought and sold goods.

It was so expensive to make, only rich people could afford to drink it. When the first chocolate shop opened in London, they added milk and sugar to make it taste sweeter.

Making chocolate

There are four main steps in making chocolate:

1. Picking and cracking Cocoa pods grow on trees. They are picked by hand and cracked open with a sharp knife. Each pod has about 20–40 beans inside.

2. Breaking down and drying
The beans are piled up under banana leaves and left for six days, to improve the flavour. Then they are laid out under the hot sun to dry.

3. Roasting and shelling The dried beans are roasted. This is when they first start to have that delicious chocolate smell! Afterwards, the hard shells are removed.

4. Crushing and mixing The inside parts of the beans are now crushed to make a liquid. Some of this is used to make cocoa butter. Different amounts of the liquid and the butter can be mixed together (with milk and sugar). This makes the three types of chocolate: milk, dark and white.

Chocolate today

All kinds of things are added to chocolate today: nuts, orange, mint, raisins and caramel. Even chilli chocolate is back in fashion!

People in Switzerland eat the most chocolate, but people in the UK also eat a lot! This chart shows how much chocolate people eat in different countries:

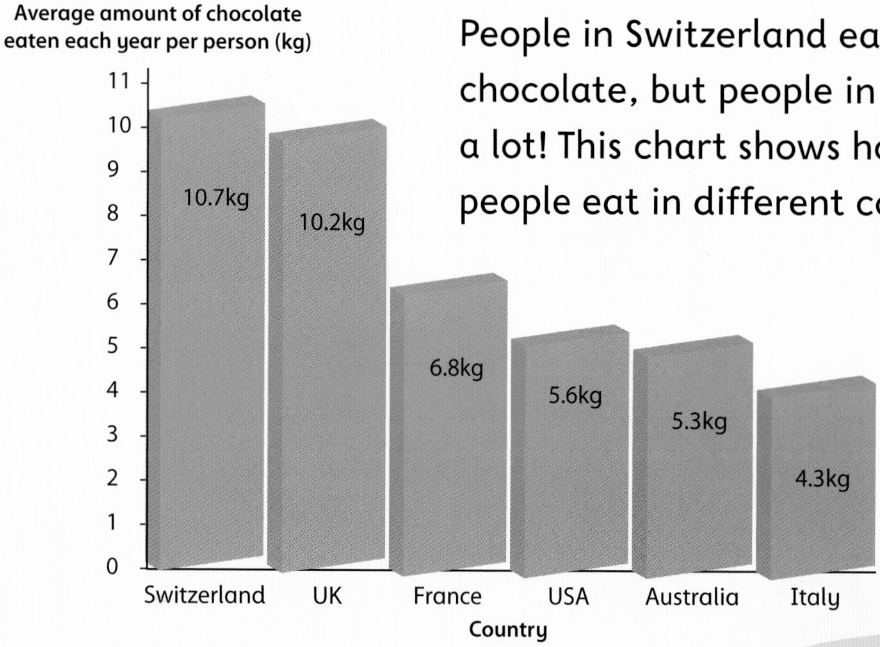

Average amount of chocolate eaten each year per person (kg)

- Switzerland: 10.7kg
- UK: 10.2kg
- France: 6.8kg
- USA: 5.6kg
- Australia: 5.3kg
- Italy: 4.3kg

Country

WARNING!

The chocolate we eat can be harmful to animals. It should never be fed to dogs or cats.

The most expensive bar of chocolate went on sale in 2009. Priced at £960, it was covered in edible gold leaf!

Chocolate and health

Doctors think that 'pure' chocolate can be good for your brain and your heart, as long as you don't eat too much, of course! You can find out how pure chocolate is by looking at the wrapper. The purest may contain over 80% cocoa.